Questions and Answers: Countries

China

by Nathan Olson

Consultant:
Xin Yang
Instructor, College of William and Mary
Williamsburg, Virginia

Capstone press

Mankato, Minnesota

Fact Finders is published by Capstone Press
151 Good Counsel Drive, P.O. Box 669, Mankato, Minnesota 56002
www.capstonepress.com

Library of Congress Cataloging-in-Publication Data
Olson, Nathan.
   China / by Nathan Olson.
   p. cm.—(Fact finders. Questions and answers. Countries)
   Includes bibliographical references.
   ISBN 0-7368-2687-4 (hardcover)
   1. China—Juvenile literature. [1. China.] I. Title. II. Series.
DS706.O48 2005
951—dc22   2003024111

Summary: A brief introduction to China, following a simple question-and-answer format to discuss land features, government, housing, transportation, industries, education, sports, art forms, holidays, food, and family life. Includes a map, fast facts, and charts.

Editorial Credits

Christine Peterson, editor; Kia Adams, series designer; Jennifer Bergstrom, book designer; maps.com, map illustrator; Wanda Winch, photo researcher; Scott Thoms, photo editor; Eric Kudalis, product planning editor

Photo Credits

Bruce Coleman Inc./Hans Reinhard, 11; Bruce Coleman Inc./James Montgomery, 15; Bruce Coleman Inc./Lee Foster, 25; Bruce Coleman Inc./M. Timothy O'Keefe, 17; Bruce Coleman Inc./Peter Jackson, 4; Capstone Press Archives, 29 (top); Corbis/AFP, 23; Corbis/Bettmann, 7; Corbis/Keren Su, 20–21; Corbis/Macduff Everton, 18–19; Cory Langley, cover (foreground); Craig Lovell, 12; Folio Inc./Walter Bibikow, 9; Photodisc/Adam Crowley, cover (background); Photodisc/John Wang, 1; Stockhaus Limited, 29 (bottom); Wolfgang Kaehler, 12–13, 20, 27

Artistic Effects

Capstone Press/Jennifer Bergstrom, 18 (Olympics logo); Ingram Publishing, 16 (notebook); Photodisc/C Squared Studios, 24 (bowl of rice and chopsticks); Photodisc/PhotoLink/Tomi, 16 (pencil)

1 2 3 4 5 6 09 08 07 06 05 04

Table of Contents

Features

Where is China?

China is a large country in east Asia. It is slightly larger than the United States. China's land size makes it the third largest country in the world.

Rivers flow across many parts of China. The Yangtze River is the world's third largest river. It flows into the East China Sea.

The Yangtze River flows across China for about 3,900 miles (6,276 kilometers). ➤

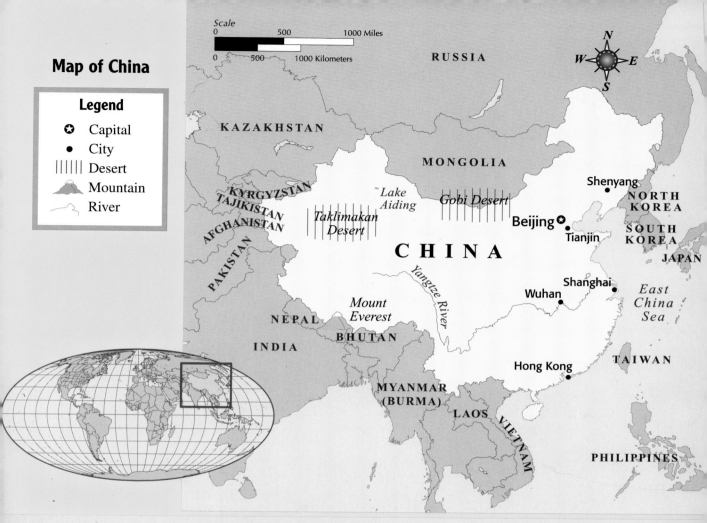

Map of China

Legend
- ✪ Capital
- • City
- ||||| Desert
- 🏔 Mountain
- 〜 River

Scale
0   500   1000 Miles
0   500   1000 Kilometers

RUSSIA

KAZAKHSTAN

MONGOLIA

Shenyang

NORTH KOREA

KYRGYZSTAN

TAJIKISTAN

AFGHANISTAN

PAKISTAN

Taklimakan Desert

Lake Aiding

Gobi Desert

Beijing ✪

Tianjin

SOUTH KOREA

JAPAN

CHINA

Yangtze River

Wuhan

Shanghai

East China Sea

NEPAL

Mount Everest

BHUTAN

INDIA

Hong Kong

TAIWAN

MYANMAR (BURMA)

LAOS

VIETNAM

PHILIPPINES

Mountains and deserts are other landforms in China. Mount Everest, the world's tallest mountain, is part of the Himalayas in southwestern China. Dry winds blow across the Gobi Desert and Taklimakan Desert.

When did China become a country?

On October 1, 1949, China became the People's Republic of China. That year, Mao Zedong and the Chinese Communist Party (CCP) took control of China. They named the country the People's Republic of China.

For thousands of years before 1949, **dynasties** ruled China. A dynasty is one family or group that rules a country. The last dynasty's rule ended in 1911. China then formed the Republic of China. The new government did not last.

Fact!

The Great Wall of China was built by many Chinese dynasties over thousands of years. Today, the wall is 4,000 miles (6,437 kilometers) long.

On October 1, 1949, Mao Zedong named China the People's Republic of China.

In the 1940s, two groups wanted to rule China. The Nationalist Party wanted a small group to lead the country. The CCP wanted people in China to work together. In 1949, the communist party won control of China.

What type of government does China have?

China is the largest country in the world with a communist government. In **communism**, the government owns all factories and land. The government shares land and money with the people.

The National People's Congress (NPC) makes laws for China. The congress meets in the capital city of Beijing. This group also chooses the president.

Fact!

Beijing was named China's capital on September 27, 1949.

China's National People's Congress meets in the Great Hall of the People in Beijing.

China's president sometimes is also the leader of the Chinese Communist Party (CCP). This party holds most government offices. China's president and congress choose a premier. The premier helps run the country.

What kind of housing does China have?

In China's large cities, most people live in apartments or small houses. Most apartments and houses have running water and electricity. Some apartments are small. Different families often share the same bathrooms and kitchens.

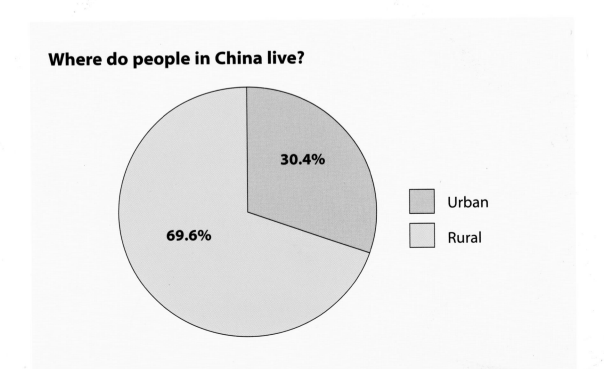

Where do people in China live?

30.4%

69.6%

Urban

Rural

In large cities like Shanghai, people often live close together in small apartments.

Most of China's people live outside the cities. They live in small houses built from mud, clay, and stone. Some houses do not have electricity or running water. **Nomads** live on China's plains. These people live in round tents called **yurts**.

What are China's forms of transportation?

People in China use different forms of transportation. In cities, many people ride bicycles. City streets are filled with people pedaling to and from work. In China's large cities, people ride subways and buses.

Railroads and rivers join most cities in China. China's railroad and river systems ship goods across the country.

Some people use carts pulled by animals to travel in China. ➤

Bicycles fill the streets in most Chinese cities. People ride bicycles to work and school.

Some parts of China do not have good roads. In these areas, people ride in carts pulled by animals. People who live in the mountains ride on horses and other animals.

China also has about 500 airports. Airplanes carry people and goods across China and around the world.

13

What are China's major industries?

One of China's major industries is mining. China's land is rich in minerals. China has more coal than any other country. People burn coal for electricity and heat.

Farming and fishing are other main industries. About half of China's people work as farmers. Rice, wheat, and tea are their main crops. China grows more rice than any country in the world. People catch fish in rivers and waters on the coast.

What does China import and export?

Imports	Exports
chemical products	clothing
machinery	coal
steel products	electronics
	rice

Workers in Chinese factories make shoes that are sent to other countries.

China's factories make many different things. Shoes, clothes, and toys are made in China. Chinese factories also make silk cloth and ceramics.

What is school like in China?

Children in China go to school for nine years. Most children begin classes at age 6. They go to six years of grade school. Most students go to high school. In rural areas, some children do not finish school. They leave school to work in fields or factories.

Fact!

In China, the school year begins in September. In January or February, students get a three-week break for the Chinese New Year. Classes end in May or June.

In China, students study many subjects. Some students also learn English.

In China, school begins with 10 minutes of exercise. Students go to classes until lunch. They take a two-hour break for lunch. During the break, they eat, play games, and even take naps. After lunch, students go to classes until 4:30 in the afternoon.

What are China's favorite sports and games?

In China, people of all ages enjoy many sports. Adults and children practice the **martial arts**. Martial arts are movements of self-defense and exercise. Many older people begin their day with **tai chi**. Tai chi is a form of exercise.

Ping-Pong, or table tennis, is China's national sport. The sport is popular. Some parks in China have Ping-Pong tables.

Fact!

In 2008, China will host the Summer Olympics in Beijing.

Ping-Pong is China's national sport. The sport is popular with people of all ages.

People in China also play many other sports and games. They play soccer and basketball. People also enjoy Chinese checkers, Chinese chess, and card games.

What are the traditional art forms in China?

Calligraphy is one of China's oldest art forms. Calligraphy is a form of writing. People paint or draw symbols to stand for words. Poetry and painting are also popular.

People in China also enjoy music, dance, and theater. They go to Chinese operas. Opera performers act out stories by singing and dancing.

Many Chinese children learn calligraphy at school. ▶

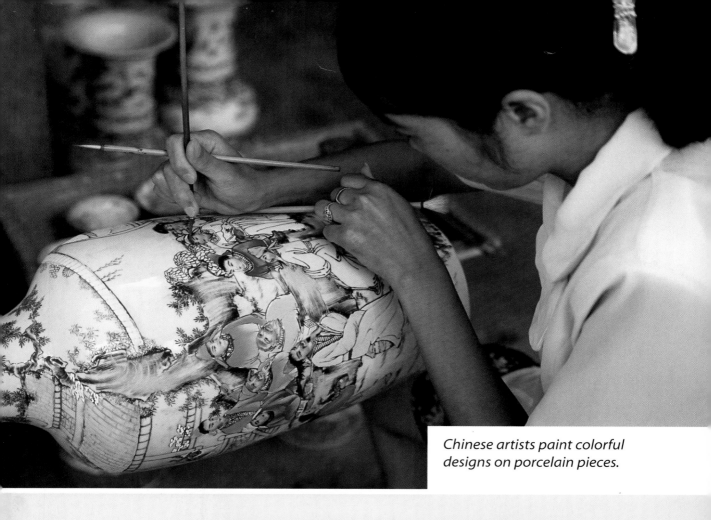

Chinese artists paint colorful designs on porcelain pieces.

Chinese **porcelain** is famous around the world. People use this pottery to make vases, dishes, and figures. People buy Chinese porcelain for its beauty.

What major holidays do people in China celebrate?

China's biggest celebration is held on October 1 in honor of National Day. This holiday marks the founding of the People's Republic of China. Parades are held in most cities. The largest parade is held in Beijing. Members of the army, dancers, and others join in the parade.

What other holidays do people in China celebrate?

Children's Day
Dragon Boat Festival
International Working Women's Day
Mid-Autumn Festival

Performers in costumes are part of most Chinese New Year celebrations.

The Chinese New Year is another popular holiday. The Chinese New Year falls in January or February. This holiday lasts 15 days. People go to parades and watch fireworks. People dressed in dragon costumes are crowd favorites.

What are the traditional foods of China?

The Chinese enjoy fresh foods, such as vegetables, chicken, and fish. Many Chinese shop at markets every day for fresh meat and vegetables. They make dumplings to serve with meals and put in soups.

In northern China, noodles are part of most meals. In southern China, meals are served with rice. Children in southern China eat a rice dish called congee.

Fact!

Chinese foods include rice, noodles, tea, dumplings, and small pastries. People in many countries enjoy Chinese foods.

Many people in China shop every day for fresh vegetables at outdoor markets.

The Chinese believe each meal helps make a healthy body. Meals are served in bowls instead of on plates. People eat food with chopsticks. They drink tea at most meals.

What is family life like in China?

Family life has changed in China. Families once had many children. In the late 1970s, the government said that families should have only one child. The law was made to control the number of people. At least 1 billion people live in China. Today, most children have no brothers or sisters.

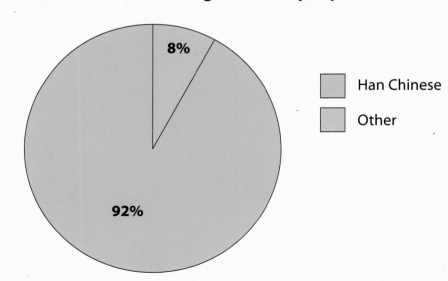

What are the ethnic backgrounds of people in China?

8%

92%

Han Chinese

Other

By law, most families in China have just one child.

In China, most families have a close relationship. Families often live together with grandparents, cousins, aunts, and uncles. Other families live near each other. Families often cook and eat meals together.

China Fast Facts

Official name:

People's Republic of China

Land area:

3,700,000 square miles
(9,583,000 square kilometers)

Average annual precipitation (Beijing):

25 inches (64 centimeters)

Average January temperature (Beijing):

24 degrees Fahrenheit
(minus 4.4 degrees Celsius)

Average July temperature (Beijing):

79 degrees Fahrenheit
(26 degrees Celsius)

Population:

1,284,303,705 people

Capital city:

Beijing

Language:

Mandarin Chinese

Natural resources:

coal, iron ore, natural gas, oil

Religions:

Christian   4%
Buddhism, Islamic, Taoism   2%

In China, 94 percent of the people
do not practice a religion.

Money and Flag

Money:

China's money is the yuan. In 2004, 1 U.S. dollar equaled about 8.28 yuans. One Canadian dollar equaled about 6.21 yuans.

Flag:

China's flag is red with a large five-point star and four smaller stars in the upper left corner. The red represents the Chinese Communist Party (CCP) coming to power in 1949. The five stars show the people of China uniting around the CCP.

Learn to Speak Mandarin Chinese

At least 90 percent of the people in China speak Mandarin Chinese. About 56,000 characters are used to write Mandarin Chinese. Use the words below to learn to speak common English words in Mandarin Chinese.

English	Mandarin Chinese	Pronunciation
hello	ni hao	(NEE HOW)
good-bye	zài jiàn	(ZEYE JEE–en)
yes	shì de	(SHEE DEE)
no	bú shì	(BOO SHEE)
please	qíng	(CHEENG)
thank you	xiè xiè	(SHEE SHEE)

Glossary

calligraphy (kuh-LIG-ruh-fee)—the art of drawing or painting words

communism (KOM-yuh-niz-uhm)—a way of organizing a country so that all the land, houses, and factories belong to the government or community, and the money and land are shared by all

dynasty (DYE-nuh-stee)—a series of rulers belonging to the same family or group

martial art (MAR-shuhl ART)—a style of fighting or self-defense that comes mostly from the Far East; people in China often practice martial arts as exercise.

nomad (NOH-mad)—a person who travels from place to place to find food and water

porcelain (POR-suh-lin)—very fine pottery often used to make vases, dishes, or figures

tai chi (TYE CHEE)—an ancient form of Chinese exercise and movement

yurt (YURT)—a circular, domed, tent made from animal skins or felt

Internet Sites

FactHound offers a safe, fun way to find Internet sites related to this book. All of the sites on FactHound have been researched by our staff.

Here's how:
1. Visit *www.facthound.com*
2. Type in this special code **0736826874** for age-appropriate sites. Or enter a search word related to this book for a more general search.
3. Click on the **Fetch It** button.

FactHound will fetch the best sites for you!

Read More

Asher, Sandy. *China.* Discovering Cultures. New York: Benchmark Books/Marshall Cavendish, 2003.

Keeler, Stephen. *China.* Changing Face of. Austin, Texas: Raintree Steck-Vaughn, 2003.

Olson, Kay Melchisedech. *China.* Many Cultures, One World. Mankato, Minn.: Capstone Press, 2003.

Index